WORKBOOK

KAY ARTHUR
DAVID ARTHUR
PETE DE LACY

HOW TO
STUDY
YOUR
BIBLE

HARVEST HOUSE PUBLISHERS
EUGENE, OREGON

Cover by Dugan Design Group, Bloomington, Minnesota

HOW TO STUDY YOUR BIBLE WORKBOOK
Copyright © 2010 by Precept Ministries International
Published by Harvest House Publishers
Eugene, Oregon 97402
www.harvesthousepublishers.com

ISBN 978-0-7369-5357-3 (pbk.)
ISBN 978-0-7369-5358-0 (eBook)

Printed in the United States of America

15 16 17 18 19 20 21 / ML-SK / 10 9 8 7 6 5 4 3 2

Contents

⬦▦▨▦⬦

PART ONE
Exercises

PART TWO
Observation Worksheets

PART THREE
Answers

Introduction

⬥⬥⬥⬥⬥

This workbook accompanies *How to Study Your Bible* and provides exercises for practicing most of the skills it describes. These exercises don't follow the book chapters point by point. Instead, they provide you with opportunities to combine the principles in the book as you practice studying the different kinds of literature found in the Bible.

Part 1 of this workbook contains the exercises. In the first four chapters, you will practice studying different kinds of literature: letters (also called epistles or correspondence), history (also called narrative), prophecy, and poetry. In each chapter, you'll find directions for applying the method to that kind of literature with either an entire book of the Bible or a section of a book. Chapter 5 deals with study skills that you can apply to any kind of literature, and chapter 6 offers review questions about the inductive study method.

In part 2 you'll find unmarked Observation Worksheets—the text of Bible passages for you to practice marking.

Part 3 of the workbook contains Observation Worksheets that we have already marked as well as our own responses to the other exercises in the book. We offer them for the sake of comparison, not because we think your responses should match ours exactly.

To benefit from this workbook, you'll need a copy of the book *How to Study Your Bible,* a Bible, colored pens or pencils, a few basic word study tools, and a blank notebook. God bless you as you take this new step in learning how to study your Bible for yourself!

Part One

EXERCISES

Letters
(Epistles, or Correspondence)

The exercises in this chapter will take you through chapters 1 through 4 of *How to Study Your Bible* as well as some of the principles in chapters 6, 11, and 12. At each step, we'll refer you to the appropriate pages of that book for your review. After completing the exercises below, you can compare your responses with ours by turning to chapter 7 of this workbook.

Before you begin the first exercise, be sure you've read through chapters 1 through 4 in *How to Study Your Bible*. We will begin by studying a letter (the book of Colossians), so the best technique is to get an overview of the book first and then dig in and study each chapter in more detail. An overview is like a pilot's view of the landscape from 10,000 feet. In the overview, we will focus on things that are obvious and important to all four chapters of Colossians. Later we'll "land the plane" and explore each chapter in more detail.

Now, because you are about to begin studying the Bible, take a moment to pray, asking God to open the eyes of your heart and help you discern truth that you can apply to your life.

Exercise 1—The Overview

1. Read through all four chapters of Colossians. On pages 29–39 of this workbook, you'll find Observation Worksheets of the entire text of Colossians in the New American Standard translation. Of course, you can use your own Bible if you prefer to work from another translation, but be prepared to mark the text extensively. Read with a purpose, asking the 5 W's and an H (who, what, when, where, why, and how) as you go. For example, how do we know that the book of Colossians is a letter? What important events or major themes stand out? Record your findings in your notebook. Don't get bogged down; you're just trying to get a feel for the general content of the book.

2. Now read Colossians again. Who is the author, who are the recipients?

Mark the author distinctively, and mark the recipients in some other way. (Remember to mark all the appropriate pronouns the same way you mark the people they point to.) For example, you could color the author blue and color the recipients red. Or you could draw a box around the author and a circle around the recipients, or you could combine color and shape. As you go, ask the 5 W's and an H so this doesn't become simply a coloring exercise. Always read with a purpose—to understand. (See *How to Study Your Bible*, pages 31–33.)

3. When you've finished marking all four chapters, look at each place you've marked references to the author. Ask the 5 W's and an H at each place, and let the text provide the answers. Make a list of everything you learn about him. Do the same for the recipients.

4. Now that you are familiar with the author and recipients, you've probably also noticed a few important events and subjects. Authors emphasize their most important ideas by repeating them. Mark these repeated key words and phrases, list them in your notebook, and record what you learn. You probably noticed that Jesus Christ is very prominent. Make sure you've marked every reference to Jesus Christ (including pronouns). Some people mark this with a red cross, but of course you can choose any symbol, color, or combination you like. In your notebook, make a list of everything you learn about Jesus in Colossians. (See *How to Study Your Bible*, pages 35–37.) Remember not to get into too much detail—we're still in the overview process.

5. Authors use various literary tools and techniques: instructions to follow, dangers to watch out for, examples to imitate, and many more. Read through Colossians again and underline or highlight any phrases that warn the Colossians against dangerous beliefs or practices.

6. Read through Colossians one more time and underline or highlight in a different color all the instructions or commands. You're looking for the good things the readers should do.

7. Now, take a moment to notice the way you've marked your Observation Worksheets. Which chapters have the most markings about Jesus? Which have the most warnings? Which have the most instructions for godly living? What relationship do you see? In other words, have you noticed a progression of thought throughout the book? Does Paul seem to have a reason for ordering his material the way he does? (Remember, we're viewing the landscape from 10,000 feet, so try to focus on the big picture!)

8. What do you think prompted Paul to write this letter to the Colossians? (This is sometimes called the occasion for writing.) Consider the analogy of a doctor recognizing a symptom, making a diagnosis, and prescribing a treatment. What problematic symptoms did Paul see in Colossae? What was his diagnosis of the root problem? What treatment did he prescribe?

9. Now you're ready to determine the main theme of Colossians. How can you summarize Paul's message to the Colossians? What's the bulk of the book about? Does a subject appear more often than any others and seem to be foundational for all the other ideas in the book? Once you've determined the main idea of the book, try to find one phrase or verse that summarizes that main idea. Use those words from the text as your theme for the book. The shorter your theme is, the easier it will be to remember. (See *How to Study Your Bible*, pages 35–36).

10. Now you can begin to build a sort of table of contents for Colossians by creating an At a Glance (AAG) chart. You'll find a blank one on page 39. The first step is to record your book theme on the top of it. Then, from what you've seen so far, what are the chapter themes? Record them. You'll complete your chart by looking for segments of the book— groupings of chapters that deal with the same topic or employ the same kind of writing. Paul commonly began his letters with a doctrinal section and then moved on to practical applications based on that truth. Do you see anything like that in Colossians? If so, divide the vertical bars into segments and label each one.

Exercise 2—Chapter Study

After you complete the overview of a letter, you're ready to study each chapter in more depth and detail. We'll use Colossians 1 as an example. You have already determined the context of the chapter—the overall flow of thought in Colossians—so in a chapter study you focus only on things that are key to that one chapter.

1. Begin your study with prayer and then read through Colossians 1, asking the 5 W's and an H. Focus on the message of this chapter. You have already marked the Observation Worksheets, noting the author, the recipients, and Jesus, and you have recorded the themes of the book and chapters on the Colossians At a Glance chart.

2. Now read through Colossians 1 again, marking all the references to God the Father and to the Holy Spirit. You marked references to Jesus Christ during the overview, but check now to see if you missed any. One way to mark God the Father is with a purple triangle shaded yellow in the center, and the Holy Spirit with a blue cloud.

3. Did you notice any key words or phrases as you read and marked? Read the chapter again, marking references to *the Word of God* and *hope*. Keep asking the 5 W's and an H as you go. Stay engaged with the text.

4. Now make lists of what you learned about Jesus, God the Father, the Holy Spirit, the Word of God, and hope. Remember that you simply look at each place you've marked these words and then write down what the text says in answer to the 5 W's and an H.

   If you had trouble determining which pronouns pointed to God the Father and which ones referred to God the Son, see chapter 16 of *How to Study Your Bible* for an introduction to a technique called *structuring*. We will practice using this tool later in this workbook.

5. When looking at a chapter in detail, always look for contrasts, comparisons, conclusions, and time references. When you find one of these, apply the 5 W's and an H to see what the author is communicating through this literary device.

    Read Colossians 1 again, looking for these devices. Mark them in any manner you choose. Some people like to mark conclusions with three dots forming a triangle, the mathematical symbol for "therefore." You might choose to draw a green clock on any time references. Think about what you learn from each.

6. Chapters are usually composed of paragraphs. Look for the paragraphs that make up Colossians 1, and discern the theme of each. Write those paragraph themes in the left margin of your Observation Worksheet. If you like, compare your themes with the ones we list on page 78.

7. Finally, review the chapter theme on your AAG chart. You can change it if you want to since you've done further study or determined the themes of the other three chapters.

Exercise 3—Interpretation: Word Studies

Good translations carry the sense of the original languages—Hebrew, Greek, and Aramaic. However, sometimes you will find an extra gem of truth by studying the meaning of a word or the grammatical construction of a sentence. Commentaries give help with some words but not all of them. Let's look at a few simple tools that will help us understand the text by revealing the meaning, mood, tense, and voice of Greek words.

1. Using online sources, a program on your computer, or printed word study tools at your disposal, look up the Greek word translated "manifested" in Colossians 1:26. Consider the definition in its various contexts: How does it fit into the verse, the paragraph, the chapter, and the book? How does this definition in these contexts increase your understanding of the word "manifested"?

2. Using online sources, a computer program, or printed word study tools at your disposal, look up the Greek verbs translated "were created" and "have been created" in Colossians 1:16 and their moods, tenses, and voices. See *How to Study Your Bible*, pages 177–192, as you consider the implications of their constructions. What is implied by the differing mood, tense, and voice combinations? In other words, what does "have been created" emphasize that "were created" does not emphasize? What is the significance of this in Paul's message to the Colossians?

2

History (Narrative)

M uch of the Bible is history, or narrative. The Old Testament has seventeen historical books, and the New Testament has four biographical and one historical book. Parts of several prophetic books, such as Jeremiah and Jonah, contain narrative as well. The principles in this chapter will help you study passages of narrative wherever it is found.

A narrative can be an account of a single event, or it can be a story that includes several events. People, places, and actions almost always figure prominently. Narratives include little if any material that directly focus on a message, unlike prophecy and correspondence. The four Gospels mix narrative (records of events) with teaching passages (exhortations, explanations, invitations, denunciations, commands, words of comfort, and other messages).

Re-read chapters 1 and 2 of *How to Study Your Bible*. When studying narrative, you don't need to do the kind of overview that a letter requires. Narratives rarely mention the author or the recipients, and they usually let the events speak for themselves about God and His ways, people and their ways, and the relationship between the two.

After completing the exercises below, you can compare your responses with ours by turning to chapter 8 of this workbook.

Exercise 1—Observation

1. Read Exodus 17 on pages 41–42, asking the 5 W's and an H as you go. In the space below, identify who the events are about, what these people are doing, how, from where, and why. You won't find answers in every verse, but you'll see them in the chapter.

    Who:

    What:

    How:

Where:

Why:

2. Who are the main characters? In narrative, the key words often refer to God and key people in the events. Read Exodus 17 again and mark *the Lord* and *Moses*.

3. List in your notebook what you learned about the Lord and Moses.

4. Note in the margin of the Observation Worksheet (or in your Bible) the key events of the chapter. These are similar to paragraph themes you noted in studying a letter. We have listed ours on page 86.

5. Determine the theme of Exodus 17. The best way to summarize what the chapter is about is usually to simply say who did what.

Exercise 2—Interpretation: Cross-Referencing

Sometimes narrative makes sense only if you read other narrative. For example, in this chapter, Moses struck a rock, and water came out. God swore to destroy Amalek. Why? What is the significance of these things?

Cross-referencing, or letting Scripture interpret Scripture, is one of the most important tools in Bible study. Concordances show many references to the word *rock*, leaving you to sort through them all to find the ones that shed light on this passage. Sometimes the cross-references in the margin or center column of your Bible are also helpful.

1. In your Bible, look up Numbers 20:1-13; Deuteronomy 8:15; Psalm 78:15-16; 1 Corinthians 10:1-6,11-13; and Hebrews 3:16-19. Note below how these passages illuminate the story in Exodus 17:1-7.

2. Using your Bible, look up Deuteronomy 25:17-19 and 1 Samuel 15:1-3. Record below what you learn about Amalek.

3

Prophecy

Prophecy is like correspondence in a few very important ways: The author usually identifies him- self and his audience and clearly communicates his message to that audience. The key to under- standing a prophetic message is often to determine when it was (or will be) fulfilled, and then we can choose the appropriate study techniques. We can learn from the circumstances of the prophet, his call, his life as he delivers his message, and his message itself. We may not be included in the proph- et's primary audience, but we can nonetheless learn about God's character and His ways.

After completing the exercises below, you can compare your responses with ours by turning to chapter 9 of this workbook.

Exercise 1—Observation, Interpretation, and Application

1. Read Jeremiah 1 on pages 43–45 and mark *the Lord* and *Jeremiah*.

2. In your notebook, make lists of what you learn about Jeremiah and the Lord.

3. Read Jeremiah 1 again and mark key words that have to do with judgment. In your notebook, list any principles you learn.

4. Determine the chapter theme.

5. Compare the names of kings with the timeline on the next page to see the historical timing.

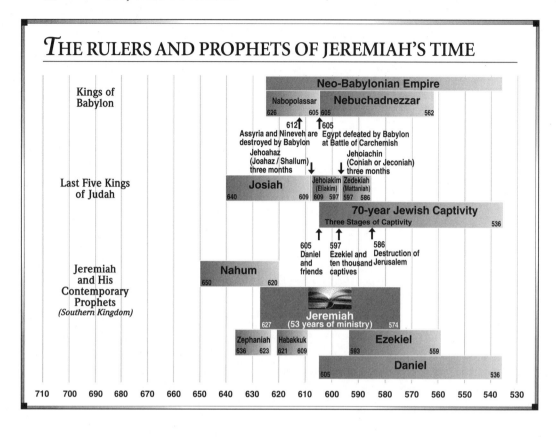

THE RULERS AND PROPHETS OF JEREMIAH'S TIME

6. How might you apply any of these principles to your own life?

Exercise 2—Observation

1. Read Amos 1 on pages 47–49 and mark *Israel* and *the Lord*.

2. Read Amos 1 again and mark any other word that is repeated enough to seem important.

3. In your notebook, make lists of the information that will help you understand the message.

4. Note the main points in the margin of the observation worksheet.

5. Determine the theme of the chapter.

6. What will happen to whom, and why? Can you determine from this chapter when this will happen? Feel free to consult the map below or a Bible atlas so you can see the relationships of these countries.

7. What does this prophecy have to do with Israel? Where are the nations located in relation to Israel? Who lived in Gilead? (Read Numbers 32:1-27 if you don't know.)

8. What is the relationship between Edom and Israel? (Read Genesis 25–27 and Obadiah if you don't know.)

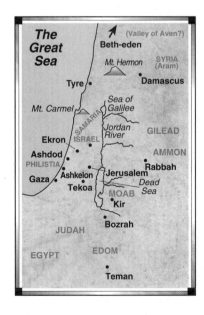

4

Poetry

Before you begin, review the characteristics of Hebrew poetry on pages 63–65 in *How to Study Your Bible*. Simply recognizing the way parallelism brings out the message is more important than identifying the specific kind of parallelism used.

After completing the exercises below, you can compare your responses with ours by turning to chapter 10 of this workbook.

Exercise 1—Observation

The psalms are Hebrew poetry. The book of Psalms is a collection of 150 individual pieces of poetry organized into five books. Like poems in a collection of English poetry, the psalms are not chapters. And the book of Psalms doesn't have one main theme, as does a letter. However, each of the psalms is an expression of worship in its own way, and all of the psalms acknowledge God's rule.

Sometimes we know the setting of a psalm by reading what appear in most English translations as superscriptions. In the Hebrew manuscripts, these are the first verse.

1. Read the superscription of Psalm 51. If you're not familiar with the story of David and Bathsheba, read 2 Samuel 11–12 and write a brief summary below. This will help you understand this psalm.

2. Now read the entire psalm. What is the tone or general sentiment?

3. Read Psalm 51 again, marking *God*, *sin* (and *transgressions*, *iniquity*, and other synonyms), and *joy*. Remember to ask the 5 W's and an H. In your notebook, list what you learn from marking each of these key words.

4. Considering the context of the psalm, what characteristics of God does David rely upon?

5. Incorporating David's own words, what contrasts do you see between God and David?

6. List five examples of parallelism in this psalm.

Exercise 2—Interpretation: Word Study

Three words in Hebrew all refer to sin. In English, they may be translated as *sin*, *iniquity*, and *transgression*. They are generally synonymous, but when they are used together, their differences are highlighted. In Psalm 51, all three are used, so a word study on each will help you understand David's admission of guilt and the depths of his remorse over his sin.

1. Using the word study tools available to you, look up the meanings of the words *iniquity* and *sin* in verse 2 and *transgression* in verse 3. For each word, write down its transliteration (the Hebrew word, using English letters) and what you learn about your relationship to God's commandments.

2. How do these three words amplify your understanding of David's view of his sin? Do you think it matches God's view of his sin?

Exercise 3—Interpretation: Cross-References

Before you can apply Scripture to your life properly, you must first interpret it correctly. In verse 11, David asks God not to take the Holy Spirit from him. Is this something we need to ask in New Testament times? The Scripture gives us the answer, but not in Psalm 51.

1. Read the following verses in your Bible and make notes:

1 Samuel 10:6-10

1 Samuel 11:6

1 Samuel 16:13-14

Jeremiah 31:31-34

Ezekiel 36:24-28

Luke 22:7,14-20

1 Corinthians 11:23-26

1 Corinthians 12:13

Ephesians 1:13-14

2. How is your relationship with the Holy Spirit different from Old Testament people's relationship with the Holy Spirit?

Exercise 4—Application

1. What cry of David do you identify with?

2. What request of his do you also make of God?

3. Does David's request that God not remove the Holy Spirit from him apply to you?

5

Structure

As you learned in *How to Study Your Bible,* analyzing thought structure helps you understand any nonnarrative writing and especially letters. Two common methods are outlining and what we call *structuring.* Robertson McQuilkin, in his book *How to Understand and Apply the Bible,* describes a technique called the *mechanical layout.* John Piper describes *arcing.* These all relate propositions to one another so you can see the way various parts of passages relate to each other. By displaying these connections, you are able to illuminate the meaning. As sentence diagramming shows how words in a sentence relate to each other, structuring shows how various thoughts relate to each other in a paragraph, a section, a chapter, or even an entire book of the Bible, especially letters.

The following exercises will give you practice in two techniques: outlining and structuring.

Exercise 1—Outlining Colossians

Read chapter 13 in *How to Study Your Bible* and then outline Colossians in your notebook. Use at least two levels. You can compare your outline with ours by turning to chapter 11 of this workbook.

Exercise 2—Structuring Jude

Like outlining, structuring illuminates the flow of thought. It shows how a thought relates to what went before and what follows. Unlike outlining, the entire text is displayed word-for-word. The text is arranged into a pattern on the page, indenting for each new sublevel of thought. This pattern shows each thought's relationship to what went before and what follows.

Read chapter 16 in *How to Study Your Bible* and then structure the rest of Jude in your notebook. To compare your structuring with ours, turn to pages 114–119 of this workbook.

Congratulations on working through these exercises! We hope that you found them helpful in practicing what you read in *How to Study Your Bible* and that the techniques make sense. As you've seen, a set of basic principles that can be applied to the five different genres of literature in the Bible.

They are like tools in a tool kit, and now you can choose the right tool for the job. You don't use all of them all the time, but you'll use some more than others because they can do many different jobs.

You might like to try one more exercise—a quiz on various principles. Use it to see how well you've grasped the method. If you don't get all the answers correct, don't stress. Just review what you missed, and you'll be on your way to a lifetime of fulfilling inductive Bible study.

And for all the exercises, remember that our answers aren't the only way to answer. The text leaves plenty of room for individual insights—including different ways to phrase things and different levels of detail—because God made us all different from one another. Check our answers in part 3 and see how you've done. We're confident you did well.

6

Review Questions
About Inductive Bible Study

This section is intended to be "closed book." Record your answers in your notebook. When you are finished, you can compare your responses with ours on pages 121–123 of this workbook.

1. What is inductive Bible study?

2. List and briefly describe the three components of inductive Bible study.

3. What is the ultimate goal of inductive Bible study?

4. What two things prepare you to do an inductive Bible study?

5. When studying a letter, how do you discover the author's purpose for writing?

6. When observing the text, what questions do you ask and why?

7. What is an overview, and when is it used?

8. How do you use an Observation Worksheet?

9. What are key words, and how do they help you understand a book?

10. What is the purpose of marking the text?

11. What is an At a Glance chart, and what are two ways to construct it?

12. Give examples of segment divisions.

13. List and describe three important techniques that can lead to proper interpretation.

14. How are word studies helpful?

15. When do you refer to commentaries?

16. Describe the difference between studying a letter and studying a narrative.

17. What are some features of prophecy?

18. Describe the important features of Hebrew poetry.

Part Two

❈ OBSERVATION WORKSHEETS ❈

Colossians I

Chapter Theme _____

1 Paul, an apostle of Jesus Christ by the will of God, and Timothy our brother,

2 To the saints and faithful brethren in Christ *who are* at Colossae: Grace to you and peace from God our Father.

3 We give thanks to God, the Father of our Lord Jesus Christ, praying always for you,

4 since we heard of your faith in Christ Jesus and the love which you have for all the saints;

5 because of the hope laid up for you in heaven, of which you previously heard in the word of truth, the gospel

6 which has come to you, just as in all the world also it is constantly bearing fruit and increasing, even as *it has been doing* in you also since the day you heard *of it* and understood the grace of God in truth;

7 just as you learned *it* from Epaphras, our beloved fellow bond-servant, who is a faithful servant of Christ on our behalf,

8 and he also informed us of your love in the Spirit.

9 For this reason also, since the day we heard *of it*, we have not ceased to pray for you and to ask that you may be filled with the knowledge of His will in all spiritual wisdom and understanding,

10 so that you will walk in a manner worthy of the Lord, to please *Him* in all respects, bearing fruit in every good work and increasing in the knowledge of God;

11 strengthened with all power, according to His glorious might, for the attaining of all steadfastness and patience; joyously

12 giving thanks to the Father, who has qualified us to share in the inheritance of the saints in Light.

13 For He rescued us from the domain of darkness, and transferred us to the kingdom of His beloved Son,

14 in whom we have redemption, the forgiveness of sins.

15 He is the image of the invisible God, the firstborn of all creation.

16 For by Him all things were created, *both* in the heavens and on earth, visible and invisible, whether thrones or dominions or rulers or authorities—all things have been created through Him and for Him.

17 He is before all things, and in Him all things hold together.

18 He is also head of the body, the church; and He is the beginning, the firstborn from the dead, so that He Himself will come to have first place in everything.

19 For it was the *Father's* good pleasure for all the fullness to dwell in Him,

20 and through Him to reconcile all things to Himself, having made peace through the blood of His cross; through Him, I say, whether things on earth or things in heaven.

21 And although you were formerly alienated and hostile in mind, *engaged* in evil deeds,

22 yet He has now reconciled you in His fleshly body through death, in order to present you before Him holy and blameless and beyond reproach—

23 if indeed you continue in the faith firmly established and steadfast, and not moved away from the hope of the gospel that you have heard, which was proclaimed in all creation under heaven, and of which I, Paul, was made a minister.

24 Now I rejoice in my sufferings for your sake, and in my flesh I do my share on behalf of His body, which is the church, in filling up what is lacking in Christ's afflictions.

25 Of *this church* I was made a minister according to the stewardship from God bestowed on me for your benefit, so that I might fully carry out the *preaching of* the word of God,

26 *that is,* the mystery which has been hidden from the *past* ages and generations, but has now been manifested to His saints,

27 to whom God willed to make known what is the riches of the glory of this mystery among the Gentiles, which is Christ in you, the hope of glory.

28 We proclaim Him, admonishing every man and teaching every man with all wisdom, so that we may present every man complete in Christ.

29 For this purpose also I labor, striving according to His power, which mightily works within me.

Colossians 2

Chapter Theme _____

1 For I want you to know how great a struggle I have on your behalf and for those who are at Laodicea, and for all those who have not personally seen my face,

2 that their hearts may be encouraged, having been knit together in love, and *attaining* to all the wealth that comes from the full assurance of understanding, *resulting* in a true knowledge of God's mystery, *that is*, Christ *Himself,*

3 in whom are hidden all the treasures of wisdom and knowledge.

4 I say this so that no one will delude you with persuasive argument.

5 For even though I am absent in body, nevertheless I am with you in spirit, rejoicing to see your good discipline and the stability of your faith in Christ.

6 Therefore as you have received Christ Jesus the Lord, *so* walk in Him,

7 having been firmly rooted *and now* being built up in Him and established in your faith, just as you were instructed, and overflowing with gratitude.

8 See to it that no one takes you captive through philosophy and empty deception, according to the tradition of men, according to the elementary principles of the world, rather than according to Christ.

9 For in Him all the fullness of Deity dwells in bodily form,

10 and in Him you have been made complete, and He is the head over all rule and authority;

11 and in Him you were also circumcised with a circumcision made without hands, in the removal of the body of the flesh by the circumcision of Christ;

12 having been buried with Him in baptism, in which you were also raised up with Him through faith in the working of God, who raised Him from the dead.

13 When you were dead in your transgressions and the uncircumcision of your flesh, He made you alive together with Him, having forgiven us all our transgressions,

14 having canceled out the certificate of debt consisting of decrees against us, which was hostile to us; and He has taken it out of the way, having nailed it to the cross.

15 When He had disarmed the rulers and authorities, He made a public display of them, having triumphed over them through Him.

16 Therefore no one is to act as your judge in regard to food or drink or in respect to a festival or a new moon or a Sabbath day—

17 things which are a *mere* shadow of what is to come; but the substance belongs to Christ.

18 Let no one keep defrauding you of your prize by delighting in self-abasement and the worship of the angels, taking his stand on *visions* he has seen, inflated without cause by his fleshly mind,

19 and not holding fast to the head, from whom the entire body, being supplied and held together by the joints and ligaments, grows with a growth which is from God.

20 If you have died with Christ to the elementary principles of the world, why, as if you were living in the world, do you submit yourself to decrees, such as,

21 "Do not handle, do not taste, do not touch!"

22 (which all *refer* to things destined to perish with use)—in accordance with the commandments and teachings of men?

23 These are matters which have, to be sure, the appearance of wisdom in self-made religion and self-abasement and severe treatment of the body, *but are* of no value against fleshly indulgence.

Colossians 3

Chapter Theme _____

1 Therefore if you have been raised up with Christ, keep seeking the things above, where Christ is, seated at the right hand of God.

2 Set your mind on the things above, not on the things that are on earth.

3 For you have died and your life is hidden with Christ in God.

4 When Christ, who is our life, is revealed, then you also will be revealed with Him in glory.

5 Therefore consider the members of your earthly body as dead to immorality, impurity, passion, evil desire, and greed, which amounts to idolatry.

6 For it is because of these things that the wrath of God will come upon the sons of disobedience,

7 and in them you also once walked, when you were living in them.

8 But now you also, put them all aside: anger, wrath, malice, slander, *and* abusive speech from your mouth.

9 Do not lie to one another, since you laid aside the old self with its *evil* practices,

10 and have put on the new self who is being renewed to a true knowledge according to the image of the One who created him—

11 *a renewal* in which there is no *distinction between* Greek and Jew, circumcised and uncircumcised, barbarian, Scythian, slave and freeman, but Christ is all, and in all.

12 So, as those who have been chosen of God, holy and beloved, put on a heart of compassion, kindness, humility, gentleness and patience;

13 bearing with one another, and forgiving each other, whoever has a complaint against anyone; just as the Lord forgave you, so also should you.

14 Beyond all these things *put on* love, which is the perfect bond of unity.

15 Let the peace of Christ rule in your hearts, to which indeed you were called in one body; and be thankful.

16 Let the word of Christ richly dwell within you, with all wisdom teaching and admonishing one another with psalms *and* hymns *and* spiritual songs, singing with thankfulness in your hearts to God.

17 Whatever you do in word or deed, *do* all in the name of the Lord Jesus, giving thanks through Him to God the Father.

18 Wives, be subject to your husbands, as is fitting in the Lord.

19 Husbands, love your wives and do not be embittered against them.

20 Children, be obedient to your parents in all things, for this is well-pleasing to the Lord.

21 Fathers, do not exasperate your children, so that they will not lose heart.

22 Slaves, in all things obey those who are your masters on earth, not with external service, as those who *merely* please men, but with sincerity of heart, fearing the Lord.

23 Whatever you do, do your work heartily, as for the Lord rather than for men,

24 knowing that from the Lord you will receive the reward of the inheritance. It is the Lord Christ whom you serve.

25 For he who does wrong will receive the consequences of the wrong which he has done, and that without partiality.

Colossians 4

Chapter Theme _____

1 Masters, grant to your slaves justice and fairness, knowing that you too have a Master in heaven.

2 Devote yourselves to prayer, keeping alert in it with an *attitude of* thanksgiving;

3 praying at the same time for us as well, that God will open up to us a door for the word, so that we may speak forth the mystery of Christ, for which I have also been imprisoned;

4 that I may make it clear in the way I ought to speak.

5 Conduct yourselves with wisdom toward outsiders, making the most of the opportunity.

6 Let your speech always be with grace, *as though* seasoned with salt, so that you will know how you should respond to each person.

7 As to all my affairs, Tychicus, *our* beloved brother and faithful servant and fellow bond-servant in the Lord, will bring you information.

8 *For* I have sent him to you for this very purpose, that you may know about our circumstances and that he may encourage your hearts;

9 and with him Onesimus, *our* faithful and beloved brother, who is one of your *number*. They will inform you about the whole situation here.

10 Aristarchus, my fellow prisoner, sends you his greetings; and *also* Barnabas's cousin Mark (about whom you received instructions; if he comes to you, welcome him);

11 and *also* Jesus who is called Justus; these are the only fellow workers for the kingdom of God who are from the circumcision, and they have proved to be an encouragement to me.

12 Epaphras, who is one of your number, a bondslave of Jesus Christ, sends you his greetings, always laboring earnestly for you in his prayers, that you may stand perfect and fully assured in all the will of God.

13 For I testify for him that he has a deep concern for you and for those who are in Laodicea and Hierapolis.

14 Luke, the beloved physician, sends you his greetings, and *also* Demas.

15 Greet the brethren who are in Laodicea and also Nympha and the church that is in her house.

16 When this letter is read among you, have it also read in the church of the Laodiceans; and you, for your part read my letter *that is coming* from Laodicea.

17 Say to Archippus, "Take heed to the ministry which you have received in the Lord, that you may fulfill it."

18 I, Paul, write this greeting with my own hand. Remember my imprisonment. Grace be with you.

Theme of Colossians:

SEGMENT
DIVISIONS

	CHAPTER THEMES
	1
	2
	3
	4

Author:

Date:

Purpose:

Key Words:

    prayer

    gospel

    wisdom

    knowledge

    all (when it
    refers to
    completeness
    or totality)

    faith

    mystery

    in Him (or
    before Him,
    through
    Him, etc.)

Exodus 17

Chapter Theme _____

1 Then all the congregation of the sons of Israel journeyed by stages from the wilderness of Sin, according to the command of the Lord, and camped at Rephidim, and there was no water for the people to drink.

2 Therefore the people quarreled with Moses and said, "Give us water that we may drink." And Moses said to them, "Why do you quarrel with me? Why do you test the Lord?"

3 But the people thirsted there for water; and they grumbled against Moses and said, "Why, now, have you brought us up from Egypt, to kill us and our children and our livestock with thirst?"

4 So Moses cried out to the Lord, saying, "What shall I do to this people? A little more and they will stone me."

5 Then the Lord said to Moses, "Pass before the people and take with you some of the elders of Israel; and take in your hand your staff with which you struck the Nile, and go.

6 "Behold, I will stand before you there on the rock at Horeb; and you shall strike the rock, and water will come out of it, that the people may drink." And Moses did so in the sight of the elders of Israel.

7 He named the place Massah and Meribah because of the quarrel of the sons of Israel, and because they tested the Lord, saying, "Is the Lord among us, or not?"

8 Then Amalek came and fought against Israel at Rephidim.

9 So Moses said to Joshua, "Choose men for us and go out, fight against Amalek. Tomorrow I will station myself on the top of the hill with the staff of God in my hand."

10 Joshua did as Moses told him, and fought against Amalek; and Moses, Aaron, and Hur went up to the top of the hill.

11 So it came about when Moses held his hand up, that Israel prevailed, and when he let his hand down, Amalek prevailed.

12 But Moses' hands were heavy. Then they took a stone and put it under him, and he sat on it; and Aaron and Hur supported his hands, one on one side and one on the other. Thus his hands were steady until the sun set.

13 So Joshua overwhelmed Amalek and his people with the edge of the sword.

14 Then the Lord said to Moses, "Write this in a book as a memorial and recite it to Joshua, that I will utterly blot out the memory of Amalek from under heaven."

15 Moses built an altar and named it The Lord is My Banner;

16 and he said, "The Lord has sworn; the Lord will have war against Amalek from generation to generation."

Jeremiah 1

Chapter Theme _____

1 The words of Jeremiah the son of Hilkiah, of the priests who were in Anathoth in the land

of Benjamin,

2 to whom the word of the Lord came in the days of Josiah the son of Amon, king of Judah,

in the thirteenth year of his reign.

3 It came also in the days of Jehoiakim the son of Josiah, king of Judah, until the end of the

eleventh year of Zedekiah the son of Josiah, king of Judah, until the exile of Jerusalem in

the fifth month.

4 Now the word of the Lord came to me saying,

5 "Before I formed you in the womb I knew you,

And before you were born I consecrated you;

I have appointed you a prophet to the nations."

6 Then I said, "Alas, Lord God!

Behold, I do not know how to speak,

Because I am a youth."

7 But the Lord said to me,

"Do not say, 'I am a youth,'

Because everywhere I send you, you shall go,

And all that I command you, you shall speak.

8 "Do not be afraid of them,

For I am with you to deliver you," declares the Lord.

9 Then the Lord stretched out His hand and touched my mouth, and the Lord said to me, "Behold, I have put My words in your mouth.

10 "See, I have appointed you this day over the nations and over the kingdoms,

To pluck up and to break down,

To destroy and to overthrow,

To build and to plant."

11 The word of the Lord came to me saying, "What do you see, Jeremiah?" And I said, "I see a rod of an almond tree."

12 Then the Lord said to me, "You have seen well, for I am watching over My word to perform it."

13 The word of the Lord came to me a second time saying, "What do you see?" And I said, "I see a boiling pot, facing away from the north."

14 Then the Lord said to me, "Out of the north the evil will break forth on all the inhabitants of the land.

15 "For, behold, I am calling all the families of the kingdoms of the north," declares the Lord; "and they will come and they will set each one his throne at the entrance of the gates of Jerusalem, and against all its walls round about and against all the cities of Judah.

16 "I will pronounce My judgments on them concerning all their wickedness, whereby they have forsaken Me and have offered sacrifices to other gods, and worshiped the works of their own hands.

17 "Now, gird up your loins and arise, and speak to them all which I command you. Do not be dismayed before them, or I will dismay you before them.

18 "Now behold, I have made you today as a fortified city and as a pillar of iron and as walls of bronze against the whole land, to the kings of Judah, to its princes, to its priests and to the people of the land.

19 "They will fight against you, but they will not overcome you, for I am with you to deliver you," declares the Lord.

Amos 1

Chapter Theme _____

1 The words of Amos, who was among the sheepherders from Tekoa, which he envisioned

in visions concerning Israel in the days of Uzziah king of Judah, and in the days of Jeroboam

son of Joash, king of Israel, two years before the earthquake.

2 He said,

"The Lord roars from Zion

And from Jerusalem He utters His voice;

And the shepherds' pasture grounds mourn,

And the summit of Carmel dries up."

3 Thus says the Lord,

"For three transgressions of Damascus and for four

I will not revoke its *punishment*,

Because they threshed Gilead with *implements* of sharp iron.

4 "So I will send fire upon the house of Hazael

And it will consume the citadels of Ben-hadad.

5 "I will also break the gate bar of Damascus,

And cut off the inhabitant from the valley of Aven,

And him who holds the scepter, from Beth-eden;

So the people of Aram will go exiled to Kir,"

Says the Lord.

6 Thus says the Lord,

"For three transgressions of Gaza and for four

I will not revoke its *punishment*,

Because they deported an entire population

To deliver *it* up to Edom.

7 "So I will send fire upon the wall of Gaza

And it will consume her citadels.

8 "I will also cut off the inhabitant from Ashdod,

And him who holds the scepter, from Ashkelon;

I will even unleash My power upon Ekron,

And the remnant of the Philistines will perish,"

Says the Lord God.

9 Thus says the Lord,

"For three transgressions of Tyre and for four

I will not revoke its *punishment*,

Because they delivered up an entire population to Edom

And did not remember *the* covenant of brotherhood.

10 "So I will send fire upon the wall of Tyre

And it will consume her citadels."

11 Thus says the Lord,

"For three transgressions of Edom and for four

I will not revoke its *punishment*,

Because he pursued his brother with the sword,

While he stifled his compassion;

His anger also tore continually,

And he maintained his fury forever.

12 "So I will send fire upon Teman

And it will consume the citadels of Bozrah."

13 Thus says the Lord,

"For three transgressions of the sons of Ammon and for four

I will not revoke its *punishment,*

Because they ripped open the pregnant women of Gilead

In order to enlarge their borders.

14 "So I will kindle a fire on the wall of Rabbah

And it will consume her citadels

Amid war cries on the day of battle,

And a storm on the day of tempest.

15 "Their king will go into exile,

He and his princes together," says the Lord.

Psalm 51

Chapter Theme _____

For the choir director. A Psalm of David, when Nathan the prophet came to him, after he had gone in to Bathsheba.

1 Be gracious to me, O God, according to Your lovingkindness;

According to the greatness of Your compassion blot out my transgressions.

2 Wash me thoroughly from my iniquity

And cleanse me from my sin.

3 For I know my transgressions,

And my sin is ever before me.

4 Against You, You only, I have sinned

And done what is evil in Your sight,

So that You are justified when You speak

And blameless when You judge.

5 Behold, I was brought forth in iniquity,

And in sin my mother conceived me.

6 Behold, You desire truth in the innermost being,

And in the hidden part You will make me know wisdom.

7 Purify me with hyssop, and I shall be clean;

Wash me, and I shall be whiter than snow.

8 Make me to hear joy and gladness,

Let the bones which You have broken rejoice.

9 Hide Your face from my sins

And blot out all my iniquities.

10 Create in me a clean heart, O God,

And renew a steadfast spirit within me.

11 Do not cast me away from Your presence

And do not take Your Holy Spirit from me.

12 Restore to me the joy of Your salvation

And sustain me with a willing spirit.

13 *Then* I will teach transgressors Your ways,

And sinners will be converted to You.

14 Deliver me from bloodguiltiness, O God, the God of my salvation;

Then my tongue will joyfully sing of Your righteousness.

15 O Lord, open my lips,

That my mouth may declare Your praise.

16 For You do not delight in sacrifice, otherwise I would give it;

You are not pleased with burnt offering.

17 The sacrifices of God are a broken spirit;

A broken and a contrite heart, O God, You will not despise.

18 By Your favor do good to Zion;

Build the walls of Jerusalem.

19 Then You will delight in righteous sacrifices,

In burnt offering and whole burnt offering;

Then young bulls will be offered on Your altar.

Part Three

❉ ANSWERS ❉

7

Letters
(Epistles, or Correspondence)

Exercise 1—The Overview

Questions 1 and 2—Marked Observation Worksheets

Colossians 1

Chapter Theme _____

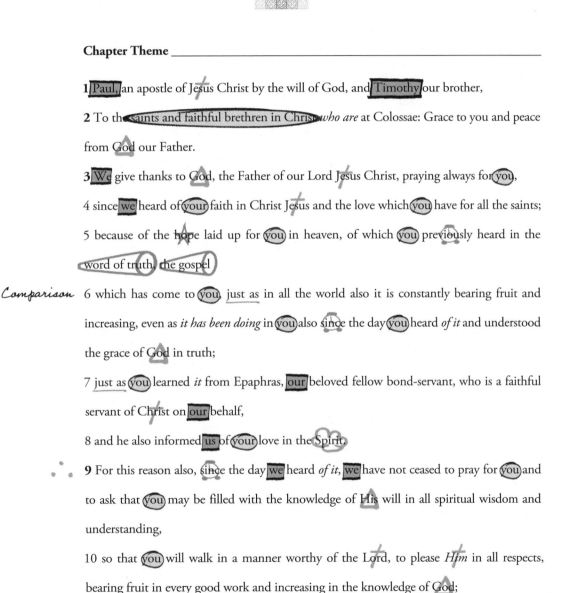

1 Paul, an apostle of Jesus Christ by the will of God, and Timothy our brother,

2 To the saints and faithful brethren in Christ who are at Colossae: Grace to you and peace from God our Father.

3 We give thanks to God, the Father of our Lord Jesus Christ, praying always for you,

4 since we heard of your faith in Christ Jesus and the love which you have for all the saints;

5 because of the hope laid up for you in heaven, of which you previously heard in the word of truth, the gospel

Comparison 6 which has come to you, just as in all the world also it is constantly bearing fruit and increasing, even as *it has been doing* in you also since the day you heard *of it* and understood the grace of God in truth;

7 just as you learned *it* from Epaphras, our beloved fellow bond-servant, who is a faithful servant of Christ on our behalf,

8 and he also informed us of your love in the Spirit.

9 For this reason also, since the day we heard *of it*, we have not ceased to pray for you and to ask that you may be filled with the knowledge of His will in all spiritual wisdom and understanding,

10 so that you will walk in a manner worthy of the Lord, to please *Him* in all respects, bearing fruit in every good work and increasing in the knowledge of God;

11 strengthened with all power, according to His glorious might, for the attaining of all steadfastness and patience; joyously

12 giving thanks to the Father, who has qualified us to share in the inheritance of the saints in Light.

13 For He rescued us from the domain of darkness, and transferred us to the kingdom of His beloved Son,

14 in whom we have redemption, the forgiveness of sins.

15 He is the image of the invisible God, the firstborn of all creation.

16 For by Him all things were created, *both* in the heavens and on earth, visible and invisible, whether thrones or dominions or rulers or authorities—all things have been created through Him and for Him.

17 He is before all things, and in Him all things hold together.

18 He is also head of the body, the church; and He is the beginning, the firstborn from the dead, so that He Himself will come to have first place in everything.

19 For it was the *Father's* good pleasure for all the fullness to dwell in Him,

20 and through Him to reconcile all things to Himself, having made peace through the blood of His cross; through Him, I say, whether things on earth or things in heaven.

21 And although you were formerly alienated and hostile in mind, *engaged* in evil deeds,

22 yet He has now reconciled you in His fleshly body through death, in order to present you before Him holy and blameless and beyond reproach—

23 if indeed you continue in the faith firmly established and steadfast, and not moved away from the hope of the gospel that you have heard, which was proclaimed in all creation under heaven, and of which I, Paul, was made a minister.

24 Now I rejoice in my sufferings for your sake, and in my flesh I do my share on behalf of His body, which is the church, in filling up what is lacking in Christ's afflictions.

25 Of *this church* I was made a minister according to the stewardship from God bestowed on me for your benefit, so that I might fully carry out the *preaching of* the word of God,

26 *that is*, the mystery which has been hidden from the *past* ages and generations, but has now been manifested to His saints,

27 to whom God willed to make known what is the riches of the glory of this mystery among the Gentiles, which is Christ in you, the hope of glory.

28 We proclaim Him, admonishing every man and teaching every man with all wisdom, so that we may present every man complete in Christ.

29 For this purpose also I labor, striving according to His power, which mightily works within me.

Colossians 2

Chapter Theme _____

1 For I want you to know how great a struggle I have on your behalf and for those who are at Laodicea, and for all those who have not personally seen my face,

2 that their hearts may be encouraged, having been knit together in love, and *attaining* to all the wealth that comes from the full assurance of understanding, *resulting* in a true knowledge of God's mystery, *that is*, Christ *Himself*,

3 in whom are hidden all the treasures of wisdom and knowledge.

4 I say this so that no one will delude you with persuasive argument.

5 For even though I am absent in body, nevertheless I am with you in spirit, rejoicing to see your good discipline and the stability of your faith in Christ.

6 Therefore as you have received Christ Jesus the Lord, *so* walk in Him,

7 having been firmly rooted *and now* being built up in Him and established in your faith, just as you were instructed, and overflowing with gratitude.

8 See to it that no one takes you captive through philosophy and empty deception, according to the tradition of men, according to the elementary principles of the world, rather than according to Christ.

9 For in Him all the fullness of Deity dwells in bodily form,

10 and in Him you have been made complete, and He is the head over all rule and authority;

11 and in Him you were also circumcised with a circumcision made without hands, in the removal of the body of the flesh by the circumcision of Christ;

12 having been buried with Him in baptism, in which you were also raised up with Him through faith in the working of God, who raised Him from the dead.

13 When you were dead in your transgressions and the uncircumcision of your flesh, He made you alive together with Him, having forgiven us all our transgressions,

14 having canceled out the certificate of debt consisting of decrees against us, which was hostile to us; and He has taken it out of the way, having nailed it to the cross.

15 When He had disarmed the rulers and authorities, He made a public display of them, having triumphed over them through Him.

16 Therefore no one is to act as your judge in regard to food or drink or in respect to a festival or a new moon or a Sabbath day—

17 things which are a *mere* shadow of what is to come; but the substance belongs to Christ.

18 Let no one keep defrauding you of your prize by delighting in self-abasement and the worship of the angels, taking his stand on *visions* he has seen, inflated without cause by his fleshly mind,

19 and not holding fast to the head, from whom the entire body, being supplied and held together by the joints and ligaments, grows with a growth which is from God.

20 If you have died with Christ to the elementary principles of the world, why, as if you were living in the world, do you submit yourself to decrees, such as,

21 "Do not handle, do not taste, do not touch!"

22 (which all *refer* to things destined to perish with use)—in accordance with the commandments and teachings of men?

23 These are matters which have, to be sure, the appearance of wisdom in self-made religion and self-abasement and severe treatment of the body, *but are* of no value against fleshly indulgence.

Colossians 3

Chapter Theme _____

1 Therefore if you have been raised up with Christ, keep seeking the things above, where Christ is, seated at the right hand of God.

2 Set your mind on the things above, not on the things that are on earth.

3 For you have died and your life is hidden with Christ in God.

4 When Christ, who is our life, is revealed, then you also will be revealed with Him in glory.

5 Therefore consider the members of your earthly body as dead to immorality, impurity, passion, evil desire, and greed, which amounts to idolatry.

6 For it is because of these things that the wrath of God will come upon the sons of disobedience,

7 and in them you also once walked, when you were living in them.

8 But now you also, put them all aside: anger, wrath, malice, slander, *and* abusive speech from your mouth.

9 Do not lie to one another, since you laid aside the old self with its *evil* practices,

10 and have put on the new self who is being renewed to a true knowledge according to the image of the One who created him—

11 *a renewal* in which there is no *distinction between* Greek and Jew, circumcised and uncircumcised, barbarian, Scythian, slave and freeman, but Christ is all, and in all.

12 So, as those who have been chosen of God, holy and beloved, put on a heart of compassion, kindness, humility, gentleness and patience;

13 bearing with one another, and forgiving each other whoever has a complaint against anyone; just as the Lord forgave you, so also should you.

14 Beyond all these things *put on* love, which is the perfect bond of unity.

15 Let the peace of Christ rule in your hearts, to which indeed you were called in one body; and be thankful.

16 Let the word of Christ richly dwell within you, with all wisdom teaching and admonishing one another with psalms *and* hymns *and* spiritual songs, singing with thankfulness in your hearts to God.

17 Whatever you do in word or deed, *do* all in the name of the Lord Jesus, giving thanks through Him to God the Father.

18 Wives, be subject to your husbands, as is fitting in the Lord.

19 Husbands, love your wives and do not be embittered against them.

20 Children, be obedient to your parents in all things, for this is well-pleasing to the Lord.

21 Fathers, do not exasperate your children, so that they will not lose heart.

22 Slaves, in all things obey those who are your masters on earth, not with external service, as those who *merely* please men, but with sincerity of heart, fearing the Lord.

23 Whatever you do, do your work heartily, as for the Lord rather than for men,

24 knowing that from the Lord you will receive the reward of the inheritance. It is the Lord Christ whom you serve.

25 For he who does wrong will receive the consequences of the wrong which he has done, and that without partiality.

Colossians 4

Chapter Theme _____

1 Masters grant to your slaves justice and fairness, knowing that you too have a Master in heaven.

2 Devote yourselves to prayer, keeping alert in it with an *attitude of* thanksgiving;

3 praying at the same time for us as well, that God will open up to us a door for the word, so that we may speak forth the mystery of Christ, for which I have also been imprisoned;

4 that I may make it clear in the way I ought to speak.

5 Conduct yourselves with wisdom toward outsiders, making the most of the opportunity.

6 Let your speech always be with grace, *as though* seasoned with salt, so that you will know how you should respond to each person.

7 As to all my affairs, Tychicus, *our* beloved brother and faithful servant and fellow bond-servant in the Lord, will bring you information.

8 *For* I have sent him to you for this very purpose, that you may know about our circumstances and that he may encourage your hearts;

9 and with him Onesimus, *our* faithful and beloved brother, who is one of your number. They will inform you about the whole situation here.

10 Aristarchus, my fellow prisoner, sends you his greetings; and *also* Barnabas's cousin Mark (about whom you received instructions; if he comes to you, welcome him);

11 and *also* Jesus who is called Justus; these are the only fellow workers for the kingdom of God who are from the circumcision, and they have proved to be an encouragement to me.

12 Epaphras, who is one of your number, a bondslave of Jesus Christ, sends you his greetings, always laboring earnestly for you in his prayers, that you may stand perfect and fully assured in all the will of God.

13 For I testify for him that he has a deep concern for you and for those who are in Laodicea and Hierapolis.

14 Luke, the beloved physician, sends you his greetings, and *also* Demas.

15 Greet the brethren who are in Laodicea and also Nympha and the church that is in her house.

16 When this letter is read among you, have it also read in the church of the Laodiceans; and you, for your part read my letter *that is coming* from Laodicea.

17 Say to Archippus, "Take heed to the ministry which you have received in the Lord, that you may fulfill it."

18 I, Paul, write this greeting with my own hand. Remember my imprisonment. Grace be with you.

COLOSSIANS AT A GLANCE

Theme of Colossians:

SEGMENT
DIVISIONS

	CHAPTER THEMES
	1
	2
	3
	4

Author:

Date:

Purpose:

Key Words:
prayer
gospel
wisdom
knowledge
all (when it
refers to
completeness
or totality)
faith
mystery
in Him (or
before Him,
through
Him, etc.)

Question 3—Key People

The Author

1:1	Paul
1:1	apostle of Jesus Christ
1:1	Timothy
1:3	gives thanks to God
1:3	always prays for them
1:4	heard of their faith in Christ and love for the saints
1:8	informed of their love by Epaphras
1:9	has not ceased to pray for them
1:12	qualified to share in inheritance
1:13	rescued from domain of darkness and transferred to the kingdom of the Son
1:14	has redemption
1:23	a minister of the gospel
1:24	rejoices in sufferings
1:24	does his share on behalf of the church
1:25	made a minister according to stewardship bestowed on him for their benefit
1:28	proclaims Christ, admonishing and teaching every man
1:29	labors for this purpose, striving according to God's power
2:1	wants them to know how great a struggle he has on their behalf
2:4	says what he does so that no one will delude them
2:5	is absent in body, with them in spirit, rejoicing
2:13	transgressions forgiven by God
2:14	freed from hostile decrees
3:4	Christ is his life
4:3	asks for prayer for an open door for the word
4:3	desires to speak forth the mystery of Christ
4:3	has been imprisoned for word

4:4   wants to make the mystery clear

4:7   affairs will be explained by Tychicus

4:8   sent Tychicus to explain circumstances and to encourage them

4:10   imprisoned with Aristarchus

4:11   has been encouraged by fellow Jewish workers

4:13   testifies to Epaphras's deep concern for them

4:18   writes a greeting with his own hand

4:18   imprisoned

The Recipients

1:2   saints and faithful brethren who are at Colossae

1:3   prayed for

1:4   have faith in Christ Jesus and love for all the saints

1:5   have hope laid up for them in heaven

1:5   have previously heard of this hope in the gospel

1:7   learned it from Epaphras

1:8   have love in the Spirit

1:9   prayed for to be filled with knowledge of God's will

1:10   to walk in manner worthy of Lord

1:12   qualified to share in inheritance of saints

1:13   rescued from domain of darkness and transferred to kingdom of the Son

1:14   have redemption, the forgiveness of sins

1:21   formerly were alienated and hostile in mind, engaged in evil deeds

1:22   reconciled in Christ's body

1:23   heard the gospel

1:27   Christ is in them

2:1   have not met Paul

2:4   Paul is concerned that they might be deluded with persuasive argument

2:5   have good discipline and stable of faith

2:6	have received Christ; admonished to walk in way they received Christ (in faith)
2:7	firmly rooted, being built up, established in their faith
2:7	were instructed in this and are to be grateful
2:10	were made complete in Christ
2:11	were circumcised in Christ
2:12	were buried with Christ in baptism and raised with Him through faith
2:13	were dead in transgressions and uncircumcision of flesh
2:13	were made alive together with Christ and forgiven
2:14	freed from hostile decrees
2:20	died with Christ but still submitting to decrees
3:1	have been raised up with Christ
3:3	have died and are hidden with Christ in God
3:4	Christ is their life
3:4	will be revealed with Christ when He is revealed
3:7	once walked in and lived in evil things
3:9	laid aside the old self
3:10	put on the new self
3:12	chosen of God; holy and beloved
3:15	called to peace of Christ and to thankfulness
3:24	will receive the reward of the inheritance; serve the Lord
4:1	have a Master in heaven
4:9	Onesimus is one of them
4:12	Epaphras is one of them

Notice that these lists focus on what we know about Paul (he uses singular pronouns, so though he mentions Timothy, Paul is the author) and about the Colossians themselves, not on what the Colossians are to do. This gives us a word picture of the author and recipients and their relationship as well as a glimpse of Paul's concerns for them. This also helps us discern why Paul wrote the letter.

Your lists may vary from ours, depending on how many observations you chose to record.

Question 4—Important Subjects

Jesus Christ

1:1	has apostles
1:3	is the Son of God, the Lord, and Christ
1:7	has servants
1:10	can be and should be pleased by our walk
1:13	rescued us, transferred us into his kingdom, and is God's Son
1:14	redemption (forgiveness of sins) is in Him
1:15	is the image of the invisible God and the firstborn of all creation
1:16	created all things in heavens and on earth; all things are through Him and for Him
1:17	is before all things and holds all things together
1:18	is head of the body, the beginning, the firstborn from the dead
1:18	is to have first place in everything
1:19	all the fullness dwells in Him
1:20	Father reconciled all things to Himself through Jesus
1:20	the blood of His cross made peace
1:22	reconciled us in His fleshly body through death
1:22	will present us before Him holy, blameless, and beyond reproach
1:24	has afflictions
1:27	Christ in you, the hope of glory—the mystery of the Gentiles
1:28	Paul proclaimed Him so every man will be complete in Him
2:2	is God's mystery
2:9	in Him all fullness of Deity dwells in bodily form
2:10	in Him you have been made complete
2:10	is the head over all rule and authority
2:11	in Him you were circumcised with a circumcision made without hands
2:12	you were buried with Him in baptism, raised with Him through faith
2:12	God raised Him from the dead

2:13   you were made alive together with Him

2:15   God triumphed over rulers and authorities through Christ

2:17   the substance belongs to Christ

3:1   is seated at the right hand of God

3:3   your life is hidden with Christ in God

3:4   will be revealed in glory

3:11   is all and in all

3:15   is the source of peace

3:16   the word of Christ

4:1   is the Master in heaven

4:12   has bondslaves

Notice in this list that the intent is to describe Christ as Paul did and not describe who we are in Christ or what we have in Christ. Look over your list and this one to see the doctrines about Christ that Paul establishes as a foundation to warn against evil and encourage godly living.

Question 5—Warnings

2:4   I say this so no one will delude you with persuasive argument.

2:8   See to it that no one takes you captive through philosophy and empty deception, according to the tradition of men, according to the elementary principles of the world, rather than according to Christ.

2:16   No one is to act as your judge in regard to food or drink or in respect to a festival or a new moon or a Sabbath day.

2:18   Let no one keep defrauding you of your prize by delighting in self-abasement and the worship of angels, taking his stand on visions he has seen.

2:20   Do not submit to decrees, such as, "Do not handle, do not taste, do not touch!"

Question 6—Commands

3:1   Keep seeking things above.

3:2   Set your mind on things above.

3:5   Consider the members of your earthly body as dead to immorality, impurity, passion, evil desire, and greed, which amounts to idolatry.

3:8   Put aside anger, wrath, malice, slander, and abusive speech.

3:9   Do not lie to one another.

3:12   Put on a heart of compassion, kindness, humility, gentleness, and patience.

3:13   Just as the Lord forgave you, so also should you forgive.

3:15   Let the peace of Christ rule in your hearts.

3:15   Be thankful.

3:16   Let the word of Christ richly dwell within you.

3:17   Do all in the name of the Lord Jesus Christ.

3:18   Wives, be subject to your husbands.

3:19   Husbands, love your wives.

3:20   Children, be obedient to your parents in all things.

3:21   Fathers, do not exasperate your children.

3:22   Slaves, in all things obey those who are your masters on earth.

4:1   Masters, grant to your slaves justice and fairness.

4:2   Devote yourselves to prayer.

4:5   Conduct yourselves with wisdom toward outsiders.

4:6   Let your speech always be with grace.

4:10   Welcome Mark.

4:15   Greet the brethren.

4:16   Have the letter read in the church of the Laodiceans.

4:16   Read the letter that is coming from Laodicea.

4:17   Say to Archippus, "Take heed to the ministry you have received in the Lord, that you may fulfill it."

4:18   Remember my imprisonment.

Question 7—Progression of Thought

Which chapter emphasizes Jesus? Which emphasizes warnings? Which emphasizes instructions for godly living? What relationship do you see?

- Chapter 1 contains basic theology about Christ and Paul's ministry purpose.

- Chapter 2 presents dangerous beliefs and practices that contradict the sound doctrine in chapter 1.

- Chapters 3 and 4 present the way to live according to the right doctrine of Christ and not according to the dangerous practices and beliefs.

Question 8—Occasion and Purpose

What do you think prompted Paul to write?

> Paul knew about the dangerous practices and beliefs that could cause the Colossian believers to go astray from sound doctrine and right living according to sound doctrine, hurting their reputation and walk, damaging their witness now and future reward.

Question 9—Main Theme

The sound doctrine about Christ should serve as the basis for the message because if believers understand and adhere to it, they can avoid the dangers, and they will be motivated to right living. Here are some suggestions for the main theme:

> Christ in You, the Hope of Glory
>
> In Him You Have Been Made Complete
>
> The Substance Belongs to Christ
>
> Christ Is All and In All

Why don't we use one of the warnings or the commands to godly living? Here's why: Paul emphasizes the truth about Christ, and he emphasizes the truth by contrasting it with falsehood and by relating the truth to godly living. The warnings and commands are all tied to truths about Christ. The focus remains on Christ—who He is, what He has done, and our future with Him. That's the motivation for avoiding the dangers and obeying the commands to godly living.

Question 10—At a Glance Chart

What are some possible chapter themes? Keep your book theme in mind, but use different themes for the chapters. Find a great phrase in each chapter—a truth, warning, or command.

Chapter 1 is mostly truths about Jesus and Paul's ministry. Does one seem to capture the message? Here are some possibilities:

> The Image of the Invisible God
>
> The Head of the Body
>
> Present Every Man Complete in Christ

Complete in Christ

Christ in You, the Hope of Glory

Chapter 2 contains the warnings, so one of those would make a good theme. Here are a few options:

Don't Be Deluded by Persuasive Argument

Don't Be Taken Captive

Let No One Judge You

Let No One Keep Defrauding You

The commands to godly living are in chapters 3 and 4, so a command would make good themes. Consider these for chapter 3:

Keep Seeking the Things Above

Let the Word of God Richly Dwell Within You

Do All in the Name of the Lord

Here are some possibilities for chapter 4:

Devote Yourselves to Prayer

Be Wise Toward Outsiders

Let Your Speech Always Be with Grace

The rest of the commands are specific to particular people, so they don't make the best chapter themes or summaries.

What possible segment divisions have you found? Here's the most obvious: Chapters 1 and 2 are doctrine, and chapters 3 and 4 are practical. Or chapter 1 is doctrine, 2 is warning, and 3 and 4 are practical commands.

Exercise 2—Chapter Study

Question 4—Lists from Colossians 1

God

    1:2   our Father

    1:2   source of grace and peace

    1:3   to be thanked

1:3   Father of our Lord Jesus Christ

1:9   has a will that can be known

1:10   can be known

1:11   glorious might strengthens us

1:12   qualified us to share in the inheritance of the saints in Light

1:13   rescued us from the domain of darkness and transferred us to the kingdom of His beloved Son

1:15   invisible

1:19   good pleasure for all fullness to dwell in Christ

1:20   good pleasure to reconcile all things to Himself through Christ

1:20   made peace through the blood of Christ's cross

1:21   reconciled you in Christ's fleshly body through death

1:25   Paul's ministry is stewardship from God

1:26   manifested mystery to His saints by His will

1:29   Paul works through God's power

Jesus Christ

1:1   has apostles

1:3   is the Son of God, the Lord, and Christ

1:7   has servants

1:10   can be and should be pleased by our walk

1:13   rescued us, transferred us into his kingdom, and is God's Son

1:14   redemption (forgiveness of sins) is in Him

1:15   is the image of the invisible God and the firstborn of all creation

1:16   created all things in heavens and on earth; all things are through Him and for Him

1:17   is before all things and holds all things together

1:18   is head of the body, the beginning, the firstborn from the dead

1:18   is to have first place in everything

1:19   all the fullness dwells in Him

1:20   Father reconciled all things to Himself through Jesus

1:20   the blood of His cross made peace

1:22   reconciled us in His fleshly body through death

1:22   will present us before Him holy, blameless, and beyond reproach

1:24   has afflictions

1:27   Christ in you, the hope of glory—the mystery of the Gentiles

1:28   Paul proclaimed Him so every man will be complete in Him

The Holy Spirit

1:8   Colossians' love is in the Spirit

The Word of God

1:5   word of truth, the gospel

1:6   bears fruit and increases

1:23   has hope in it

1:23   has been proclaimed in all creation under heaven

1:25   Paul's ministry to preach the Word of God

Hope

1:5   laid up for us in heaven

1:5   learned about in the gospel

1:23   hope of the gospel was proclaimed in all creation under heaven

1:23   Paul a minister of the hope of the gospel

1:27   Christ in you, the hope of glory

Questions 5—Comparisons, Contrasts, and Conclusions in Colossians 1

Just as is a marker for comparison, so in verse 6 we see that the gospel came to the Colossians "just as" it came to the rest of the world—bearing fruit and increasing. We also see in verse 7 how the Colossians learned it—"just as" from Epaphras.

The kingdom of darkness is contrasted with the kingdom of God's beloved Son in verse 13. Verses 21 and 22 contain another contrast: The Colossians were formerly alienated and hostile in mind and engaged in evil deeds, but now they are reconciled. Another contrast is in verse 26: The mystery was hidden from the past ages and generations but is now manifested.

Chapter 1 contains several time phrases: *formerly, now, previously, since the day,* and *past ages and generations.*

The word *therefore* does not appear in this chapter, but the phrase *for this reason* does, and it too points to a conclusion—based on what went before, something in particular will happen. So in verse 9, we see that since Paul heard of the Colossians' fruitful reception of the gospel, he has continued to pray that they will be filled with the knowledge of God's will.

Question 6—Paragraph Themes in Colossians 1

Paragraph 1 (verse 1): Paul and Timothy

Paragraph 2 (verse 2): To the Saints at Colossae

Paragraph 3 (verses 3-8): Thanks to God for Your Reception of the Gospel

Paragraph 4 (verses 9-14): May You Continue to Grow

Paragraph 5 (verses 15-20): The Image of the Invisible God

Paragraph 6 (verses 21-23): God Reconciled You

Paragraph 7 (verses 24-29): Proclaiming the Mystery of Christ

Your themes need not match ours exactly, but these serve as examples of how themes can convey the main points of the paragraphs succinctly using words from the text. You don't have to invent anything or use cute phrases or paraphrases. If you use the text, you'll remember more of Scripture.

Question 7—Chapter Theme

Here are some options:

The Image of the Invisible God

The Head of the Body

Present Every Man Complete in Christ

Complete in Christ

Christ in You, the Hope of Glory

Exercise 3—Interpretation: Word Studies

Question 1—Manifested

Strong's number 5319, *phaneroo*—to make visible or known that which has been hidden or unknown, whether by words or other means. To cause to be seen, disclosed.

You can see that the context (had been hidden) is the key. The mystery is now made known or disclosed. In this case, it was manifested by preaching of the gospel, and we know who made it known—God.

Question 2—Were Created and Have Been Created

Were created—Strong's number 2936, *ektisthe* or *ktizo*—create, produce from nothing. The aorist indicative indicates an action occurring in the past without regard to time duration. The passive voice shows that the things were acted upon—Jesus created them.

Have been created—same Greek word, but the tense, mood, and voice are perfect indicative passive. In the indicative mood, the perfect tense emphasizes the continuing result of an action completed in the past. The English "have been" tries to convey this sense. It wasn't created just *through* Jesus in the past, but *for* Him in the past and *for* Him even to the present. It is His now.

8

History (Narrative)

Exercise 1—Observation

Marked Observation Worksheets

Exodus 17

Chapter Theme _____

1 Then all the congregation of the sons of Israel journeyed by stages from the wilderness of Sin, according to the command of the Lord, and camped at Rephidim, and there was no water for the people to drink.

Quarrel over water Massah & Meribah

2 Therefore the people quarreled with Moses and said, "Give us water that we may drink." And Moses said to them, "Why do you quarrel with me? Why do you test the Lord?"

3 But the people thirsted there for water; and they grumbled against Moses and said, "Why, now, have you brought us up from Egypt, to kill us and our children and our livestock with thirst?"

4 So Moses cried out to the Lord, saying, "What shall I do to this people? A little more and they will stone me."

5 Then the Lord said to Moses, "Pass before the people and take with you some of the elders of Israel; and take in your hand your staff with which you struck the Nile, and go.

6 "Behold, I will stand before you there on the rock at Horeb; and you shall strike the rock, and water will come out of it, that the people may drink." And Moses did so in the sight of the elders of Israel.

7 He named the place Massah and Meribah because of the quarrel of the sons of Israel, and because they tested the Lord, saying, "Is the Lord among us, or not?"

Battle with Amalek

8 Then Amalek came and fought against Israel at Rephidim.

9 So Moses said to Joshua, "Choose men for us and go out, fight against Amalek. Tomorrow I will station myself on the top of the hill with the staff of God in my hand."

10 Joshua did as Moses told him, and fought against Amalek; and Moses, Aaron, and Hur went up to the top of the hill.

11 So it came about when Moses held his hand up, that Israel prevailed, and when he let his hand down, Amalek prevailed.

12 But Moses hands were heavy. Then they took a stone and put it under him, and he sat on it; and Aaron and Hur supported his hands, one on one side and one on the other. Thus his hands were steady until the sun set.

13 So Joshua overwhelmed Amalek and his people with the edge of the sword.

The Lord is My Banner 14 Then the Lord said to Moses, "Write this in a book as a memorial and recite it to Joshua, that I will utterly blot out the memory of Amalek from under heaven."

15 Moses built an altar and named it The Lord is My Banner;

War against Amalek 16 and he said, "The Lord has sworn; the Lord will have war against Amalek from generation to generation."

Question 1—The 5 W's and an H

The First Story

> Who: the congregation of the sons of Israel
>
> What: journeyed
>
> How: according to the command of the Lord
>
> Where: from the wilderness of Sin to Rephidim
>
> Why: the command of the Lord

The Second Story

> Who: Moses
>
> What: held up his staff during battle with Amalek
>
> How: with help from Aaron and Hur
>
> Where: on a hill
>
> When: until the sun set
>
> Why: the command of the Lord

Question 3—Lists About the Lord and Moses

The Lord

> 17:1   commanded the people to journey to Rephidim
>
> 17:2,7 tested by the people who wondered if God was with them
>
> 17:4-6 answered Moses' cry
>
> 17:6   stood before Moses to produce water from a rock
>
> 17:9   gave Moses a staff
>
> 17:14   directed Moses to write the story of Amalek's defeat in a book as a memorial that He will blot out memory of Amalek.
>
> 17:15   The LORD is My Banner
>
> 17:16   swore to have war against Amelek from generation to generation

Moses

17:2   people quarreled with him

17:2   asked why the people quarreled with him and tested the Lord

17:3   the people grumbled against him because of thirst

17:4   cried out to Lord for help; feared he would be stoned

17:6   obeyed the Lord and struck the rock with the staff

17:9   told Joshua to choose men to fight Amalek

17:10 went with Aaron and Hur to top of a hill

17:11 held staff up

17:12 hands were heavy, so Aaron and Hur helped him until the sun set

17:15 built an altar and name it The Lord is My Banner

Question 4—Key Events in Exodus 17

Quarreling and grumbling because of thirst

Moses strikes the rock

Massah and Meribah

Joshua's battle with Amalek

Aaron and Hur support Moses

The Lord is My Banner and war with Amalek

Question 5—Chapter Theme

Water from the rock and the battle with Amalek

Note that you can combine major events. You don't have to choose just one unless it's really the main event. In this case, the two events use about the same number of verses.

Exercise 2—Interpretation: Cross-Referencing

Question 1—Water from the Rock

In Numbers 20:1-13, water again comes from a rock, but this time at the Wilderness of Zin. Moses was to speak to the rock, but he struck the rock with his rod the same way he did the first time. Water came out, but God said he and Aaron didn't believe and wouldn't lead the people into the Promised Land.

These events are celebrated in Deuteronomy 8:15 and Psalm 78:15-16.

In 1 Corinthians 10:1-6,11-13, Paul applies these accounts to Jesus and the church. The people were drinking a spiritual drink from a spiritual rock, Christ. These things happened as examples for us. We don't have to succumb to temptation.

Hebrews 3:17-19 explains that the people died because of unbelief.

Question 2—Amalek

In Deuteronomy 25:17-19, as the people were preparing to enter the land, Moses reminded them to blot out the memory of Amalek because Amalek attacked the Israelite stragglers at the rear when they were faint and weary. The Amalekites did not fear God.

In 1 Samuel 15:1-3, Samuel delivers God's instructions to King Saul. He was to destroy Amalek. God remembered his original command, and centuries later prompted Israel to remember and obey.

9

Prophecy

Exercise 1—Observation, Interpretation, and Application

Marked Observation Worksheets

Jeremiah 1

Chapter Theme _____

1 The words of (Jeremiah) the son of Hilkiah, of the priests who were in Anathoth in the land

of Benjamin,

2 to whom the word of the Lord came in the days of Josiah the son of Amon, king of Judah,

in the thirteenth year of his reign.

3 It came also in the days of Jehoiakim the son of Josiah, king of Judah, until the end of the

eleventh year of Zedekiah the son of Josiah, king of Judah, until the exile of Jerusalem in

the fifth month.

4 Now the word of the Lord came to me saying,

5 "Before I formed you in the womb I knew you,

And before you were born I consecrated you;

I have appointed you a prophet to the nations."

6 Then I said, "Alas, Lord God!

Behold I do not know how to speak,

Because I am a youth."

7 But the Lord said to me,

"Do not say, 'I am a youth,'

Because everywhere I send you, you shall go,

And all that I command you, you shall speak.

8 "Do not be afraid of them,

For I am with you to deliver you," declares the Lord.

9 Then the Lord stretched out His hand and touched my mouth, and the Lord said to me,

"Behold, I have put My words in your mouth.

10 "See, I have appointed you this day over the nations and over the kingdoms,

To pluck up and to break down,

To destroy and to overthrow,

To build and to plant."

11 The word of the Lord came to me saying, "What do you see, Jeremiah?" And I said, "I see a rod of an almond tree."

12 Then the Lord said to me, "You have seen well, for I am watching over My word to perform it."

13 The word of the Lord came to me a second time saying, "What do you see?" And I said, "I see a boiling pot, facing away from the north."

14 Then the Lord said to me, "Out of the north the evil will break forth on all the inhabitants of the land.

15 "For, behold, I am calling all the families of the kingdoms of the north," declares the Lord; "and they will come and they will set each one his throne at the entrance of the gates of Jerusalem, and against all its walls round about and against all the cities of Judah.

16 "I will pronounce My judgments on them concerning all their wickedness, whereby they have forsaken Me and have offered sacrifices to other gods, and worshiped the works of their own hands.

17 "Now, gird up your loins and arise, and speak to them all which I command you. Do not be dismayed before them, or I will dismay you before them.

18 "Now behold, I have made you today as a fortified city and as a pillar of iron and as walls of bronze against the whole land, to the kings of Judah, to its princes, to its priests and to the people of the land.

19 "They will fight against you, but they will not overcome you, for I am with you to deliver you," declares the Lord.

Question 2—Lists from Jeremiah 1

The Lord

1:2	word came to Jeremiah in thirteenth year of Josiah's reign
1:5	knew Jeremiah before He formed him in the womb
1:5	consecrated Jeremiah before he was born
1:7	told Jeremiah not to say "I am a youth"
1:7	will send Jeremiah
1:8	with Jeremiah to deliver him
1:9	touched Jeremiah's mouth and put His words in his mouth
1:10	appointed Jeremiah over the nations and kingdoms to pluck up and break down, to destroy and overthrow, to build and plant
1:11	gives Jeremiah a vision of an almond tree rod
1:12	watching over His word to perform it
1:13	sent word to Jeremiah again with vision of boiling pot
1:14	interprets the vision—evil will break forth out of the north
1:15	calling all the families of the kingdoms of the north to come against Jerusalem
1:16	pronounces judgment against Jerusalem and Judah, who have forsaken Him and sacrificed to other gods
1:17	commands Jeremiah to speak His words
1:17	will dismay Jeremiah if he is dismayed
1:18	made Jeremiah a fortified city, pillar of iron, and wall of bronze against land, kings, princes, priests, and people.
1:19	with Jeremiah to deliver him

Jeremiah

1:1	son of Hilkiah, of the priests from Anathoth in Benjamin
1:4	word of Lord came to him in thirteenth year of Josiah's reign
1:5	formed by God in womb, known by God before that, consecrated by God before he was born, appointed a prophet to the nations
1:6	does not know how to speak, is a youth
1:7	will be sent by God, and will go and speak what God commands

1:8   God is with him to deliver him

1:9   God put His words in his mouth

1:10   appointed over the nations and kingdoms to pluck up and break down, destroy and overthrow, build and plant

1:11   shown a vision of a rod of an almond tree

1:12   saw well

1:13   shown a vision of a boiling pot facing north

1:17   told not to be dismayed

1:18   made a fortified city, pillar of iron, and walls of bronze, to land, kings, princes, priests, and people

1:19   God will be with him

As you can see, there's a lot of overlap in these lists because of the dialogue between God and Jeremiah—what God says and shows Jeremiah and what Jeremiah hears and sees.

Question 3—Principles of Judgment

pluck up, break down, destroy and overthrow nations and kingdoms

boiling pot facing away from the north

evil to break forth on land of Judah

kingdoms of north come against Jerusalem and cities of Judah

God's judgments on Israel concerning their wickedness whereby they have forsaken Him and offered sacrifices to, worshiped other gods

Question 4—Chapter Theme

Jeremiah is appointed by God

Question 6—Application of Principles

What God did for Jeremiah, He does for us. He forms us, knows us, consecrates us, appoints us, empowers us, protects us, and delivers us.

Exercise 2—Observation

Marked Observation Worksheet

Amos I

❖◇❖◇❖

Chapter Theme _____

Words of Amos 1 The words of (Amos) who was among the sheepherders from Tekoa, which he envisioned

in visions concerning Israel in the days of Uzziah king of Judah, and in the days of Jeroboam

son of Joash, king of Israel, two years before the earthquake.

2 (He) said,

"The Lord roars from Zion

And from Jerusalem He utters His voice;

And the shepherds' pasture grounds mourn,

And the summit of Carmel dries up."

Prophecy against 3 Thus says the Lord,

Damascus "For three transgressions of Damascus and for four

I will not revoke its *punishment*,

Because they threshed Gilead with *implements* of sharp iron.

4 "So I will send fire upon the house of Hazael

And it will consume the citadels of Ben-hadad.

5 "I will also break the gate bar of Damascus,

And cut off the inhabitant from the valley of Aven,

And him who holds the scepter, from Beth-eden;

So the people of Aram will go exiled to Kir,"

Says the Lord.

Prophecy against Gaza

6 Thus says the Lord,

"For three transgressions of Gaza and for four

I will not revoke its *punishment*,

Because they deported an entire population

To deliver *it* up to Edom.

7 "So I will send fire upon the wall of Gaza

And it will consume her citadels.

8 "I will also cut off the inhabitant from Ashdod,

And him who holds the scepter, from Ashkelon;

I will even unleash My power upon Ekron,

And the remnant of the Philistines will perish,"

Says the Lord God.

Prophecy against Tyre

9 Thus says the Lord,

"For three transgressions of Tyre and for four

I will not revoke its *punishment*,

Because they delivered up an entire population to Edom

And did not remember *the* covenant of brotherhood.

10 "So I will send fire upon the wall of Tyre

And it will consume her citadels."

Prophecy against Edom

11 Thus says the Lord,

"For three transgressions of Edom and for four

I will not revoke its *punishment*,

Because he pursued his brother with the sword,

While he stifled his compassion;

His anger also tore continually,

And he maintained his fury forever.

12 "So I will send fire upon Teman

And it will consume the citadels of Bozrah."

Prophecy against Ammon

13 Thus says the Lord,

"For three transgressions of the sons of Ammon and for four

I will not revoke its *punishment*,

Because they ripped open the pregnant women of Gilead

In order to enlarge their borders.

14 "So I will kindle a fire on the wall of Rabbah

And it will consume her citadels

Amid war cries on the day of battle,

And a storm on the day of tempest.

15 "Their king will go into exile,

He and his princes together," says the Lord.

Question 3—List of what you learned from marking that helps you understand the message.

The Lord

1:2	roars from Zion
1:2	utters his voice from Jerusalem
1:3	will not revoke punishment of Damascus for transgressions
1:4	will send fire on house of Hazael
1:4	will consume the citadels of Ben-hadad
1:5	will break the gate bar of Damascus
1:5	cut off inhabitant from valley of Aven
1:5	cut off him who holds the scepter
1:5	people of Aram will go exiled to Kir
1:6	will not revoke punishment of Gaza
1:7	will send fire upon wall of Gaza to consume citadels
1:8	will cut off inhabitant from Ashdod
1:8	will cut off him who hold the scepter from Ashkelon
1:8	will unleash His power upon Ekron
1:9	will not revoke punishment of Tyre
1:10	will send fire on wall of Tyre and consume citadels
1:11	will not revoke punishment of Edom
1:12	will send fire on Teman and consume citadels of Bozrah
1:13	will not revoke punishment of Ammon
1:14	will kindle a fire on wall of Rabbah and consume her citadels
1:15	their king will go into exile

You can see the repetition and pattern of judgment on several nations. The pattern includes fire to consume citadels, and nations, cities, and kings are involved. But how are these connected to Israel?

The repeated phrase is "for three transgressions and four." So you might make a list about the transgressions of each.

Transgressions

1:3   Damascus threshed Gilead with implements of sharp iron.

1:6   Gaza deported an entire population to deliver it up to Edom.

1:9   Tyre delivered up an entire population to Edom and did not remember the covenant of brotherhood.

1:11 Edom (another name for Esau and his descendants) pursued his brother (Jacob and his descendants) with the sword while he stifled his compassion. His anger also tore continually and he maintained his fury forever.

1:13 Ammon ripped open the pregnant women of Gilead in order to enlarge their borders.

Question 4—Main Points

Words of Amos

Prophecy against Damascus

Prophecy against Gaza

Prophecy against Tyre

Prophecy against Edom

Prophecy against Ammon

Question 5—Chapter Theme

The Punishment of Israel's Enemies

Question 6—What Will Happen to Whom?

1:4-5 Damascus will be burned, and its inhabitants will be cut off and sent into exile.

1:7-8 Gaza will be burned, and her inhabitants will be cut off.

1:10 Tyre will be burned.

1:11 Edom will be burned.

1:13 Ammon will be burned and exiled.

Question 7—The Connection to Israel

The nations surrounded Israel and were Israel's enemies. Reuben, Gad, and the half-tribe of Manasseh settled east of the Jordan River in Gilead and Bashan.

Question 8—Edom and Israel

Edom is the nation that descended from Esau, Jacob's brother, who sold his birthright and lost his blessing. Esau hated Jacob, who was later renamed Israel. Obadiah said that the nation of Edom gloated over Jerusalem's destruction.

10

Poetry

Exercise 1—Observation

Question 1—Context: The Superscription

> David sinned by committing adultery with Bathsheba and having her husband, Uriah,
> killed. Nathan confronted David with his sin, and David and Bathsheba's child died
> as an infant.

Question 2—Tone

> Remorse, grief over sin

Question 3—Marking the Text and Making Lists

Psalm 51

Chapter Theme _____

For the choir director. A Psalm of David, when Nathan the prophet came to him, after he had

gone in to Bathsheba.

1 Be gracious to me, O God, according to Your lovingkindness;

According to the greatness of Your compassion blot out my transgressions.

2 Wash me thoroughly from my iniquity

And cleanse me from my sin.

3 For I know my transgressions,

And my sin is ever before me.

4 Against You, You only, I have sinned

And done what is evil in Your sight,

So that You are justified when You speak

And blameless when You judge.

5 Behold, I was brought forth in iniquity,

And in sin my mother conceived me.

6 Behold, You desire truth in the innermost being,

And in the hidden part You will make me know wisdom.

7 Purify me with hyssop, and I shall be clean;

Wash me, and I shall be whiter than snow.

8 Make me to hear joy and gladness,

Let the bones which You have broken rejoice.

9 Hide Your face from my sins

And blot out all my iniquities.

10 Create in me a clean heart, O God,

And renew a steadfast spirit within me.

11 Do not cast me away from Your presence

And do not take Your Holy Spirit from me.

12 Restore to me the joy of Your salvation

And sustain me with a willing spirit.

13 *Then* I will teach transgressors Your ways,

And sinners will be converted to You.

14 Deliver me from bloodguiltiness, O God, the God of my salvation;

Then my tongue will joyfully sing of Your righteousness.

15 O Lord, open my lips,

That my mouth may declare Your praise.

16 For You do not delight in sacrifice, otherwise I would give it;

You are not pleased with burnt offering.

17 The sacrifices of God are a broken spirit;

A broken and a contrite heart, O God, You will not despise.

18 By Your favor do good to Zion;

Build the walls of Jerusalem.

19 Then You will delight in righteous sacrifices,

In burnt offering and whole burnt offering;

Then young bulls will be offered on Your altar.

God

> 51:1   gracious according to lovingkindness
>
> 51:1   able to blot out transgressions
>
> 51:1   compassionate
>
> 51:4   justified when speaks
>
> 51:4   blameless when He judges
>
> 51:6   desires truth in the innermost being
>
> 51:6   will make me know wisdom in hidden part
>
> 51:8   has "broken David's bones"
>
> 51:10   can create a clean heart and renewed spirit
>
> 51:11   can cast David away and take the Holy Spirit from him
>
> 51:13   transgressors and sinners can be converted to God
>
> 51:14   delivers from guilt
>
> 51:14   is Savior
>
> 51:15   controls David's lips
>
> 51:16   does not delight in sacrifice or burnt offering
>
> 51:17   accepts the sacrifice of a broken spirit
>
> 51:17   will not despise a broken and contrite heart
>
> 51:18   His favor can do good to a people
>
> 51:19   delights in righteous sacrifices

Sin (Transgressions, Iniquity)

> 51:2   makes one unclean, calls for cleansing
>
> 51:3   can be ever before one
>
> 51:4   sin is against God
>
> 51:5   we are brought forth in iniquity
>
> 51:5   we are conceived in sin
>
> 51:9   sin offends God, but can be blotted out by Him
>
> 51:13   sinners can be taught God's ways and converted

Joy

    51:8   God is source of joy

    51:12 He can restore it

    51:14 tongue can joyfully sing of God's righteousness when delivered from guilt

Question 4—Character of God

grace

lovingkindness

compassion

justice

righteousness

Question 5—Contrast Between David and God

In contrast to God's character above, David was created in sin and has sinned. He needs cleansing and restoration, and only God can do that. David realizes his sin is against God and must turn to God for that. He knows that God is just in judging his sin based on His righteousness, but he asks for grace for his unrighteousness based on God's lovingkindness and compassion.

Question 6—Parallelism

Wash me thoroughly from my iniquity
Cleanse me from my sin

I know my transgressions
My sin is ever before me

Purify me with hyssop and I shall be clean
Wash me and I shall be whiter than snow

Make me hear joy and gladness
Let the bones which You have broken rejoice

Hide Your face from my sins
Blot out all my iniquities

You do not delight in sacrifice
You are not pleased with burnt offering

You will delight in righteous sacrifices,
In burnt offerings and whole burnt offering;
Then young bulls will be offered on Your altar.

Exercise 2—Interpretation: Word Study

Question 1—Meanings of Iniquity, Sin, and Transgression

- *sin*—Strong's number 2403, *chattah*—failure to meet a standard; assumes there is a standard

- *iniquity*—Strong's number 5771, *avon*—perversity, depravity, a twisting or perverting of a standard

- *transgression*—Strong's number 6588, *pesha*—rebellion against a standard

Question 2—David's View of Sin

David sees himself as not meeting God's standard, but rebelling against it and perverting it. And yet he asks for God's grace, based on God's character and his own confession and contrition.

Exercise 3—Interpretation: Cross-References

Question 1—The Holy Spirit

1 Samuel 10:6-10—The Spirit of God came on Saul mightily, and he prophesied.

1 Samuel 11:6—The Spirit of God came on Saul when he heard of the Ammonites' attack on Jabesh.

1 Samuel 16:13-14—When Samuel anointed David, the Spirit of the Lord came on David mightily, but the Spirit of the Lord left Saul.

Jeremiah 31:31-34—God will make a new covenant with Israel and Judah. He will write His law on their heart, they will all know Him, and He will forgive their iniquity and sin.

Ezekiel 36:24-28—God will put a new heart and a new Spirit in Israel.

Luke 22:7,14-20—At the Last Supper, Jesus inaugurates the new covenant with disciples.

1 Corinthians 11:23-26—This new covenant is for all believers.

1 Corinthians 12:13—All believers are baptized into one body by the Spirit and made to drink of one Spirit.

Ephesians 1:13-14—Believers are sealed in Christ with Holy Spirit of promise as pledge of our inheritance with view of redemption.

Question 2—The Holy Spirit in the Old and New Testaments

In the Old Testament, the Holy Spirit came upon prophets and kings but then left them. In the New Testament, all believers are permanently sealed with the Holy Spirit.

Question 4—Application

David's Cry

David's Request

Application to You

These two have no right answer, but typical responses have to do with forgiveness of sin, a clean heart, a steadfast spirit, the joy of salvation, and the like.

11

Structure

Exercise 1—Outlining Colossians

Christ Is All and in All

I. Complete in Christ

    A. Greetings from Paul and Timothy to the Colossians

    B. Prayer of thanks for the Colossians' faith

    C. Prayer for growth in wisdom and understanding

    D. Christ is the image of the invisible God

    E. You were once alienated but are now reconciled

    F. Paul was made a minister of the word of God

II. See To It No One Takes You Captive

    A. Don't be deluded by persuasive argument

    B. Don't be taken captive through philosophy and empty deception

    C. Don't let anyone judge you regarding food and drink or festivals

    D. Don't let anyone keep defrauding you of your prize

    E. Don't submit to decrees

III. Keep Seeking the Things Above

    A. Set your mind on things above

    B. Consider earthly body as dead

    C. Put aside anger, wrath, malice, slander, and abusive speech

    D. Do not lie to one another

    E. Put on a heart of compassion

    F. Forgive

    G. Put on love

    H. Let the peace of Christ rule in your hearts

    I. Let the word of Christ richly dwell in you

    J. Do all in the name of the Lord

    K. Instructions to groups

        1. Wives, be subject to husbands

        2. Husbands, love your wives

        3. Children, be obedient to parents

        4. Fathers, do not exasperate children

        5. Slaves, obey your masters on earth

        6. Masters, grant to your slaves justice and fairness

IV. Gracious Speech

    A. Devote yourselves to prayer

    B. Conduct yourselves with wisdom toward outsiders

V. Closing Personal Comments

    A. Tychicus will bring you information about my affairs

    B. Welcome Aristarchus

    C. Epaphras sends his greetings

    D. Luke sends his greetings, and Demas

    E. Greet the brethren

    F. Have this letter read to Laodicean church

    G. Read my letter from Laodicea

    H. Say to Archippus "take heed to your ministry to fulfill it"

    I. Paul writes a greeting with his own hand

    J. Remember my imprisonment

This outline can have other sublevels depending on how detailed you want it to be. In fact, you can outline entire book word for word if you so desire. For example, under the greeting from Paul and Timothy, merely add the details given about Paul, Timothy, and the Colossians.

A. Greetings from Paul and Timothy to the Colossians

    1. Paul is an apostle of Jesus Christ by the will of God

    2. Timothy is Paul's brother

    3. The Colossians are saints and faithful brethren

    4. Paul and Timothy wish grace and peace to the Colossians

This is simply an example of how to use an outline to see the flow of thought in a letter.

Exercise 2—Structuring Jude

1:1

Jude

   a bond-servant of Jesus Christ

   and

   brother of James

To those who are the called

       beloved in God the Father

       and

       kept for Jesus Christ

1:2

May mercy

   and

   peace

   and

   love   be multiplied to you

1:3

Beloved

   while I was making every effort to write you

         about our common salvation

I felt the necessity to write to you

      appealing that you contend earnestly for the faith

            which was once for all handed down to the saints

1:4

    For certain persons have crept in unnoticed

      those who were long beforehand marked out for this condemnation

    ungodly persons

       who turn the grace of our God into licentiousness

         and

         deny our only Master and Lord

            Jesus Christ

1:5
Now
I desire to remind you
 though you know all things once for all
 that the Lord
  after saving a people out of the land of Egypt
  subsequently destroyed those who did not believe

1:6
 And
  angels who did not keep their own domain
   but
   abandoned their proper abode
 He has kept
  in eternal bonds
  under darkness
  for the judgment of the great day

1:7
  Just as Sodom
   and
   Gomorrah
   and
   the cities around them
    since they
     in the same way as these
     indulged in gross immorality
     and
     went after strange flesh
    are exhibited as an example
     in undergoing the punishment of eternal fire

1:8
Yet

    in the same way

these men

        also by dreaming

        defile the flesh

        and

        reject authority

        and

        revile angelic majesties

1:9
But

Michael the archangel

    when he disputed with the devil

        and

            argued about the body of Moses

did not dare pronounce against him a railing judgment

    but

    said "The Lord rebuke you"

1:10
But

these men revile the things which they do not understand

and

    the things which they know by instinct

        like unreasoning animals

    by these things

they are destroyed

1:11
Woe to them!

For they have gone the way of Cain

    and

        for pay

they have rushed headlong into the error of Balaam

and

perished in the rebellion of Korah

1:12

These are the men who are hidden reefs in your love feasts

when they feast with you without fear

caring for themselves

clouds without water

carried along by winds

autumn trees without fruit

doubly dead

uprooted

1:13

wild waves of the sea

casting up their own shame like foam

wandering stars

for whom the black darkness has been reserved forever

1:14

It was also about these men *that* Enoch

in the seventh generation from Adam

prophesied saying "Behold

the Lord came with many thousands of His holy ones

1:15

to execute judgment upon all

and

to convict all the ungodly

of all their ungodly deeds

which they have done in an ungodly way

and

of all the harsh things

which ungodly sinners have spoken against Him"

1:16 These are grumblers
    finding fault
    following after their *own* lusts
they speak arrogantly
    flattering people for the sake of *gaining an* advantage

1:17 But
you beloved ought to remember the words
    that were spoken beforehand by the apostles of our Lord Jesus Christ
        that *they were* saying to you

1:18   "In the last time
          there will be mockers
            following after their own ungodly lusts"

1:19 These are the ones who cause divisions
    worldly-minded
    devoid of the Spirit

1:20 But
you beloved
    building yourselves up on your most holy faith
    praying in the Holy Spirit

1:21 keep yourselves in the love of God
    waiting anxiously for the mercy of our Lord Jesus Christ to eternal life

1:22
And
have mercy on some who are doubting
1:23
save others
   snatching them out of the fire
and
have mercy on some
   with fear hating even the garment polluted by the flesh

1:24
Now
to Him who is able to keep you from stumbling
   and
   to make you stand in the presence of His glory
      blameless with great joy

1:25
   to the only God our Savior
   through Jesus Christ our Lord
be glory
   majesty
   dominion
   and
   authority
      before all time
      and
      now
      and
      forever
Amen

12

Review Questions About
Inductive Bible Study

1. What is inductive Bible study?

   Studying the Bible directly and first as the primary source, and consulting other people's teachings secondarily.

2. Define the three components of inductive Bible study.

   Observation—seeing what the text says

   Interpretation—understanding what the text means

   Application—making truth relevant to our lives, whether beliefs or actions

3. What is the ultimate goal of inductive Bible study?

   A transformed life.

4. What two things prepare you to do an inductive Bible study?

   Prayer and reading the text.

5. When studying a letter, how do you discover the author's purpose for writing?

   Observe what you learn about the author, his situation, the recipients, their situation, and the author's use of repetition to emphasize his instruction.

6. When observing the text, what questions do you ask and why?

   Who, what, when, where, why, and how. They help us read with a purpose.

7. What is an overview, and when is it used?

In a letter, it's getting the big picture of the book as a whole. It is performed before digging into individual chapters in detail.

8. How do you use an Observation Worksheet?

By observing carefully, marking words, and looking for contrasts, comparisons, and the like. Also by using the marked items to determine paragraph and chapter themes, make lists, and so on.

9. What are key words, and how do they help you understand a book?

They are words that the author repeats or emphasizes in some other way. They unlock the meaning of the text.

10. What is the purpose of marking the text?

Marking helps the reader slow down, become immersed in the text, and read with a purpose. It highlights repetition and emphasis and gives a visual cue for determining themes and making lists.

11. What is an At a Glance chart, and what are two ways to construct it?

Like a table of contents, it lists chapter themes and the book theme, highlighting important topics or events in a book. It also has segment divisions to show the structure of a book and common ideas across chapters.

In a letter, it is constructed during the overview, before studying chapters. In other kinds of literature, the chapter themes are listed as each chapter is studied, and then it is completed at the end of the study by adding segments and the book theme.

12. Give examples of segment divisions.

Paul's letters often begin with a doctrinal section and end with a section of practical application. Historical books include segments about common characters or events.

13. List and describe three important techniques that can lead to proper interpretation.

Cross-references—letting Scripture interpret Scripture.

Word studies—understanding word meanings and grammar.

Context—keeping meanings in context of what's around them.

Letting the clear, repeated teaching inform the obscure or single reference.

14. How are word studies helpful?

> Sometimes nuances of meaning are lost in translation of individual words. Also, Greek and Hebrew grammar does not always translate exactly into English.

15. When do you refer to commentaries?

> Last, after doing your own study.

16. Describe the difference between studying a letter and studying a narrative.

> Letters usually have an author, recipients, an occasion for writing, and a purpose. Historical narrative centers around characters and events that take place. The focus is not teaching doctrine or themes, but events that show God's character and right or wrong behaviors.

17. What are some features of prophecy?

> Prophecy often has historical narrative, characters, and events. But it usually includes a message that corrects some issue, often a message of judgment. It reveals God's character as He judges and offers restoration. Messages include redemption and hope.

18. Describe the important features of Hebrew poetry.

> Parallelism and acrostic forms. Psalm 119 is an acrostic, part of Lamentations is an acrostic. Parallelism can be synonymous, synthetic, or antithetic, among others, using different words that communicate the same idea, a contrasting idea, or an expansion of an idea.

NOW AVAILABLE IN
NASB® & ESV®

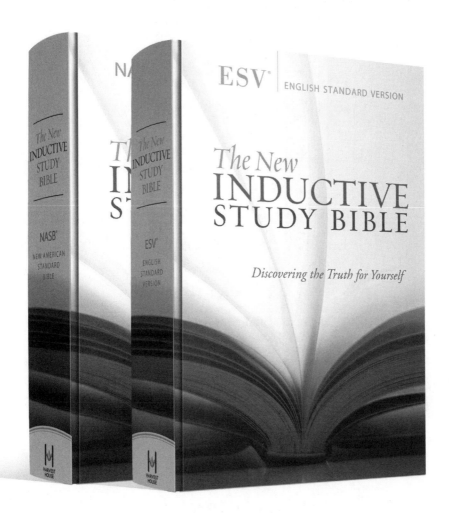

The Gold Medallion–winning *New Inductive Study Bible* (over 700,000 sold) is now available in the trusted English Standard Version. This Bible is based entirely on the inductive study approach, leading readers directly back to the source and allowing God's Word to become its own commentary.

Also available in Milano Softone™ and Genuine Leather!

For more information, visit www.precept.org/store.
Make sure to check out Inductive Bible Study Training opportunities!

Harvest House Books
by Kay Arthur

Discover the Bible for Yourself

God, Are You There?

God, How Can I Live?

God, I Need Your Comfort

How to Study Your Bible

How to Study Your Bible Workbook

Israel, My Beloved

Lord, I Need Answers

Lord, Teach Me to Pray in 28 Days

Lord, Teach Me to Study the Bible in 28 Days

A Marriage Without Regrets

A Marriage Without Regrets Study Guide

Powerful Moments with God

Speak to My Heart, God

Teach Me Your Ways

Youniquely Woman
(with Emilie Barnes and Donna Otto)

BRING THE WHOLE COUNSEL OF GOD'S WORD TO KIDS!

▼ GENESIS
God's Amazing Creation (Genesis 1–2)
Digging Up the Past (Genesis 3–11)
Abraham, God's Brave Explorer (Genesis 11–25)
Extreme Adventures with God (Genesis 24–36)
Joseph, God's Superhero (Genesis 37–50)

 ## ◀ 2 TIMOTHY
Becoming God's Champion

 ## ◀ JAMES
Boy, Have I Got Problems!

ESTHER ▶
God Has Big Plans for You, Esther

 ## ◀ REVELATION
Bible Prophecy for Kids
(Revelation 1–7)
A Sneak Peek into the Future
(Revelation 8–22)

DANIEL ▶
You're a Brave Man, Daniel!
(Daniel 1–6)
Fast-Forward to the Future
(Daniel 7–12)

▲ TOPICAL & SKILLS
God, What's Your Name? (Names of God)
Lord, Teach Me to Pray (for Kids)
How to Study Your Bible (for Kids)
also available in DVD
Cracking the Covenant Code (for Kids)

JONAH ▶
Wrong Way, Jonah!

◀ GOSPEL OF JOHN
Jesus in the Spotlight (John 1–10)
Jesus—Awesome Power, Awesome Love (John 11–16)
Jesus—To Eternity and Beyond (John 17–21)

BOOKS IN THE
NEW INDUCTIVE STUDY SERIES